FROM FARM TO FORK

Where Do Vegetables Come From?

Linda Staniford

capstone

Edited by Helen Cox Cannons
Designed by Steve Mead
Original illustrations © Capstone Global Library Limited 2016
Illustrated by Steve Mead
Picture research by Tracy Cummins
Production by Victoria Fitzgerald
Originated by Capstone Global Library Limited

Library of Congress Cataloging-in-Publication Data
Names: Staniford, Linda, author. | Staniford, Linda. From farm
to fork.
Title: Where do vegetables come from? / by Linda Staniford.
Other titles: Heinemann read and learn.
Description: Chicago, Illinois : Heinemann-Raintree, [2017] |
Series: From farm to fork | Series: Heinemann read and learn |
Includes bibliographical references and index.
Identifiers: LCCN 2015043859| ISBN 9781484633519 (library
binding) | ISBN 9781484633557 (pbk.) | ISBN 9781484633595
(ebook pdf)
Subjects: LCSH: Carrots—Juvenile literature. | Vegetables—
Juvenile literature.
Classification: LCC SB351.C3 S83 2017 | DDC 635/.13--dc23

Acknowledgments
The author and publisher are grateful to the following for
permission to reproduce copyright material: Alamy: JTB
MEDIA CREATION Inc. 13, Paula Solloway, 15; Getty
Images: Caspar Benson, 14, Jamie Grill, 21, Kevin Horan, 12;
iStockphoto: jfmdesign, 17, SolStock, 20; Shutterstock: Adisa,
4, Amnarj Tanongrattana, 19, Audrius Merfeldas, Cover Back,
8, Casther, 11, Deep OV, 22 Top Middle, Denis and Yulia
Pogostins, 10, Diana Taliun, 22 Top, Egor Rodynchenko, 22
Bottom Middle, Elena Elisseeva, 5, Iasmina Calinciuc, 16,
itsmejust, Cover Left, K.Decha, 9, Kalin Eftimov, 22 Middle,
Monkey Business Images, 7, MSPhotographic, Cover Right,
Noam Armonn, 6, ribeiroantonio, 22 Bottom, Taina
Sohlman, 18.

Every effort has been made to contact copyright holders
of material reproduced in this book. Any omissions will
be rectified in subsequent printings if notice is given to
the publisher.

Some words are shown in bold, **like this**. You can find out
what they mean by looking in the glossary.

Table of Contents

What Are Vegetables?

There are many different kinds of vegetables. Vegetables are good for us to eat.

Vegetables give us **vitamins** and **minerals**. Vitamins and minerals keep our bodies healthy.

Where Do Vegetables Grow?

Vegetables grow all over the world. They grow on farms. The farms can be large or small.

You can even grow your own vegetables.
In this book we will look at how carrots
get from farms to your plate.

Where Do Carrots Come From?

Carrots grow from seeds. The seeds are sowed in the spring.

The carrot seeds are planted in rows
in the soil. The farmer waters the soil to
keep it damp.

How Do Carrots Grow?

The carrot seeds soon start to grow.
Leaves sprout up above the soil.

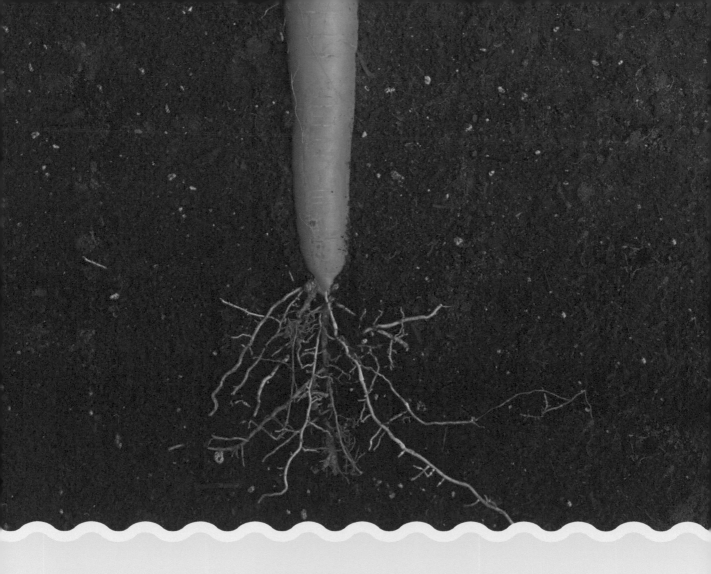

Under the ground, the roots of the carrot grow downward. The carrot becomes bigger and thicker.

How Are Carrots Harvested?

Harvesting is when the farmer collects the ripe vegetables. The carrots are ready to be harvested in the summer.

On large farms, the farmer uses a special machine to dig the carrots out of the ground. On small farms, the carrots are dug up by hand.

What Happens to the Carrots After Harvesting?

After the carrots have been **harvested**, the leaves are cut off. Taking the leaves off keeps the carrots fresh for longer.

The carrots are washed so that soil is taken off them. They are sorted into different sizes and put into bags.

How Are Carrots Preserved?

Preserving is treating vegetables to stop them from going bad. Carrots can be **frozen** to preserve them. First, they are cooked in hot water for a short time. Then, they are cooled very fast.

Carrots can also be canned. Many kinds of vegetables can be preserved in this way.

What Happens to the Carrots Next?

The bags of carrots are packed into trucks. The trucks take the carrots to supermarkets and other stores.

In the stores, workers put the carrots out in the produce section. There are a lot of other vegetables to choose from, too.

How Do Carrots Get to Our Table?

When we go grocery shopping, we can choose the vegetables we like to eat. Many people like to eat carrots.

Carrots can be eaten cooked or **raw**.
The carrots have come a long way from
farm to fork!

All Kinds of Vegetables!

There are many types of vegetable. Carrots, potatoes, parsnips, and radishes are all root vegetables. They are called root vegetables because they are the part of the plant that grows under the ground.

Other vegetables come from different parts of a plant. Celery is the stem. Beans and peas are seeds. Broccoli and cauliflowers are baby flowers that have not yet opened!

Glossary

frozen become solid or icy after being put in a very low temperature

harvest pick a crop

minerals substances found in some foods that help our bodies stay healthy

preserve keep something fresh

raw uncooked and unprocessed

vitamins good things in foods that help our bodies stay healthy

Find Out More

Books

Dickmann, Nancy. *Food from Farms* (World of Farming). Chicago: Heinemann Library, 2011.

Rooney, Anne. *Carrots Grow Under the Ground* (What Grows in My Garden). Mankato, Minn.: QEB, 2013.

Internet sites

Facthound offers a safe, fun way to find Internet sites related to this book. All of the sites on Facthound have been researched by our staff.

Here's all you do:
Visit www.facthound.com
Type in this code: 9781484633519

Index